HOW CHRISTMAS BEGAN

Dianne Bates

Illustrated by Linda Forss

The
CHRISTMAS COLLECTION

First published 1990 by
THE MACMILLAN COMPANY OF AUSTRALIA PTY LTD
107 Moray Street, South Melbourne 3205
6 Clarke Street, Crows Nest 2065

Associated companies and representatives throughout the world

National Library of Australia cataloguing in publication data

Bates, Dianne 1948-
  How Christmas began.

Includes index.
ISBN 0 7329 0214 2.

1. Jesus Christ - Nativity - Juvenile literature.
2. Christmas - History - Juvenile literature. I. Forss,
Linda. II. Title. (Series: Christmas collection).

232.921

Set in Plantin by Graphicraft Typesetters
Printed in Hong Kong

CONTENTS

Luke, 2

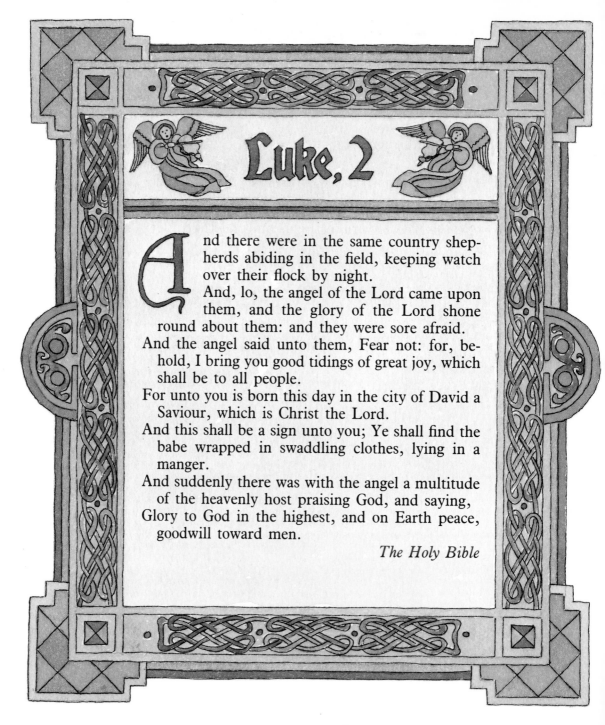

And there were in the same country shepherds abiding in the field, keeping watch over their flock by night.

And, lo, the angel of the Lord came upon them, and the glory of the Lord shone round about them: and they were sore afraid.

And the angel said unto them, Fear not: for, behold, I bring you good tidings of great joy, which shall be to all people.

For unto you is born this day in the city of David a Saviour, which is Christ the Lord.

And this shall be a sign unto you; Ye shall find the babe wrapped in swaddling clothes, lying in a manger.

And suddenly there was with the angel a multitude of the heavenly host praising God, and saying,

Glory to God in the highest, and on Earth peace, goodwill toward men.

The Holy Bible

1. THE MEANING OF CHRISTMAS

Christmas means so much to people all over the world. It is a time of gift-giving, tree-decorating, carol-singing and feasting. For Christians of all races and denominations, it is a religious holiday, a day of festivities, of family reunions and of hope for a peaceful and prosperous new year. But, above all, Christmas carries with it the message of peace and goodwill that was begun two thousand years ago with the birth of Jesus Christ.

Almost all that is known about the birth of Jesus is told in brief passages in The Bible by the disciples Luke and Matthew. Without them, there would be no Christmas. Many of our customs and symbols are connected with the Christmas stories the disciples told. Originally, Christians exchanged greetings during the Christmas season. Soon they came to exchange gifts, perhaps as a symbol of the Three Wise Men who gave gold, frankincense and myrrh to the Christ Child. The bright star on top of the Christmas tree represents the star which guided them to Bethlehem. And the Christmas tree reminds people that Christ, like the evergreen tree in the midst of winter, brings life and hope for us all.

The origins of our Christmas festivities go back a long way, even before Christ's birth, to pagan festivals and ceremonies. Following the birth of Christ, the early Christians set about converting the pagans to Christianity. One way they did this was by merging pagan celebrations with the Christmas story. Over the centuries, new customs came into being and blended with the old. This is how Christmas, as we know it today, came to be celebrated.

2. THE FIRST CHRISTMAS

The Journey to Bethlehem and Christ's Birth

Mary was a Jewish girl – most likely about sixteen – living two thousand years ago in the village of Nazareth in Palestine. One day a messenger from God, the angel Gabriel, came to visit her. This is the message that he brought:

"Behold, you will bear a son whose name shall be called Jesus. He will grow up to be called the Son of God, the Saviour of all people and King for ever and ever."

In the same village lived Joseph, a carpenter. He was puzzled when told of the angel's visit. But he loved Mary so he married her and promised to always protect her and her unborn child.

At that time Palestine was ruled by the Romans. The Roman Emperor, Augustus Caesar, ordered that all people should go to the town of their ancestors to be counted for a census. Joseph, who was descended from King David, had to go to the city of David, Bethlehem. The distance from Nazareth to Bethlehem was one hundred and forty-four kilometres – a long, hard, four-day journey – but Mary and Joseph must have been pleased to go. The prophet Micah had foretold that the future ruler of Israel would come from Bethlehem. Now, thanks to the Emperor's order, their child would be born there.

Across the cold desert Mary and Joseph travelled, Mary riding a donkey and Joseph walking beside her. There were many other families travelling to Bethlehem for the census, and when at last they reached the town it was late and they could find nowhere to stay. They asked at an inn, but it was crowded. Someone, perhaps the innkeeper, suggested that they might find shelter in a stable nearby.

Christmas crib scenes often show a wooden stable, but it is more likely the stable was a cave. This is where they found shelter.

One night not long after, the child was born as the angel Gabriel had told and Mary wrapped him in swaddling cloths and laid him in a manger. The manger, a feeding trough for animals, made a perfect crib for the newborn baby.

The Shepherds

Bethlehem lay on the edge of a vast, semi-desert plain. Groups of shepherds lived on the plain, tending flocks of sheep. Shepherds of that time were rough, dirty men, poorly paid and despised. Nevertheless, they were the first people chosen to hear the joyful news of the birth of the Son of God. Luke tells us an angel of the Lord appeared to them and the glory of the Lord shone around them and they were filled with fear.

The angel told the shepherds not to be afraid, that they should go to Bethlehem where they would find the "Saviour, which is Christ the Lord". The angel mentioned the manger, a clue that the shepherds should search for the newborn baby not in the houses of Bethlehem, but in its stables. The Gospel tells us that they "went with haste, and found Mary and Joseph, and the babe", lying, as the angels had foretold, "in the manger". The shepherds were overjoyed that the angel's message was true and they knelt and worshipped the baby. Then they went back to their sheep, telling everyone on their way of the wonder they had seen.

Shepherds still keep flocks of sheep near Bethlehem. Over the centuries the location of the birthplace has been passed down by word of mouth. In AD 326, most of the Romans had become Christian and the Emperor of the time, Constantine, built a basilica over the place where it is believed Christ was born. The basilica is still there, one of the oldest Christian churches in the world.

The Magi

In an Eastern land far from Bethlehem – probably Arabia – were three wise men, or "Magi", who were expecting the birth of the King of the Jews. The Magi were astrologers who watched the night skies carefully, for they believed the future could be foretold in the stars. Tradition turned the Wise Men into three kings and gave them names. But all this is legend. The disciple Matthew who told about the Wise Men in the Gospels did not give this information. The names of the men – Caspar, Melchior and Balthazar – were first mentioned in an Armenian story written in the sixth century.

When the stars said the time was right, the Magi travelled to Jerusalem. It was a long trek and they arrived some months after the birth of Christ. At once they began to say to the townspeople: "Where is he who has been born King of the Jews? For we have seen his star in the East, and have come to worship him." This must have alarmed the Jews for the only king they had was Herod, a brutal ruler whose palace was in Jerusalem. These foreigners were asking dangerous questions. Herod had already ordered the murders of members of his family, as well as other people. If he heard of another king being born, he might fly into a rage and order his death. In fact, this is what happened.

Herod summoned the Wise Men secretly and found out from them what time the star appeared. Then he sent them to Bethlehem saying: "Go and search diligently for the child, and when you have found him bring me word, that I too may come and worship him."

It was not far from Jerusalem to Bethlehem. The star which the Magi had seen in the East showed them the way. When the Magi saw the star had come to rest, they fell down and worshipped the Christ Child. The treasures they gave Jesus, gold, frankincense and myrrh, were typical of Eastern people who would have thought it rude to pay a visit to a superior without offering gifts. Frankincense and myrrh – resins used in perfumes – were rare and precious.

The Magi must have stayed in Bethlehem for only a short time because they were warned in a dream not to return to Herod. Joseph also received a warning, and the Holy Family left the village too. Seeking a place where they would be safe from Herod, they travelled south towards Egypt. The gold the Magi gave would have come in handy on this long trip.

It was just as well Joseph and his family fled when they did, for soon after Herod killed all the male children in Bethlehem who were under the age of two. He did this hoping to destroy the infant king before he could become a threat to Herod's throne. In some countries today, December 28 is set aside to honour the Holy Innocents, the children killed by Herod.

3. WHEN WAS CHRIST BORN?

No one knows the exact date and year of the birth of Christ. The Bible does not give us any clue and no record was handed down. In the early days of Christianity there was no celebration of Christ's birth.

In the sixth century a monk named Dionysius Exiguus (Dennis the Little) made the calculation that became the basis for our calendar. Dionysius started from the year AD 1 which he believed was the year Christ was born. However, later studies revealed that Christ was probably born several years earlier than that.

It is not likely either, that Jesus was born on December 25. Christ's Mass – or Christmas as it soon became known – was first celebrated in the year 354. The Church chose the official date. One reason was that the middle of winter – December – seemed a good time for a holiday as the cold weather prevented people from working outdoors.

Long before Christmas there had been many mid-winter pagan festivals. The Church knew if it arranged the celebration of Christmas at this time, people would still keep pagan traditions. They decided to allow pagan festivals to remain, but to give them Christian meaning. Many of the things that we look on as being part of our Christmas celebrations today have their origin in these earlier festivities.

According to the Roman calendar, December 25 was the date of the winter solstice. This marked the middle of winter. After this date, the days grew longer and warmer until spring came, bringing with it new life. December 25 was a public holiday for the Romans. It was known as the birthday of the unconquered sun. Today we celebrate it as the birthday of the Son of God who brought new life and hope to the world.

4. THE FESTIVAL OF SATURNALIA

For centuries the Romans celebrated a holiday called Saturnalia in honour of Saturn, their god of agriculture. Saturnalia was a lively, joyful celebration, similar in many ways to our modern Christmas.

During the seven-day festival, slaves were given temporary freedom. No one worked and people could do as they liked. For example, gambling was forbidden by Roman law but it was allowed during Saturnalia. The courts were shut down and schools were closed.

Gifts were exchanged, usually candles and little dolls called *sigillaria*. Sometimes money was given. The rich put on lavish feasts where a "king" was chosen to take charge of the fun. People crowded the streets, singing, dancing, eating, drinking and sometimes wearing costumes with animal heads. Torchlight processions wound through the city streets and plays were performed.

In the New Year festivities, gifts were again exchanged. The earliest presents were green branches. As the Roman Empire and Roman customs spread, the greenery came to include ivy, holly and firs, which are used in today's celebrations of Christmas.

13

5. THE BOY BISHOP, THE FESTIVAL OF FOOLS AND THE LORD OF MISRULE

In pagan times during Saturnalia (which ended on December 25), Roman masters would change places with their slaves, even waiting on them. This tradition was carried over into Christian festivities.

In the Middle Ages, the Church selected a "boy bishop". He was usually a choirboy who was treated exactly as a real bishop would be.

For the duration of the holiday, he wore the Bishop's robes, led a procession in his honour and preached sermons (though he did not celebrate Mass).

Another celebration was the Festival of Fools. A clergyman was chosen to lead the festivities. He was given the title of archbishop, cardinal or even pope and was allowed to give commands to everyone. Sometimes his commands were quite rude!

In the King's court, a Lord of Misrule was in charge of holiday activities. His every command had to be obeyed. In time, his real job became to arrange elaborate pageants called *masques* and to make sure everyone enjoyed the twelve days of the festive season.

Just as the holiday was celebrated in the Roman Saturnalia festival, so Christians made eating, drinking, gambling and wearing masks part of their Christmas fun.

6. THE FIRST CRÈCHE

Some people in the Middle Ages were worried that Christmas was in danger of being swamped by pagan festivities. One who decided to do something about this was Francis of Assisi. An Italian nobleman who had founded the Franciscans, a religious order dedicated to serving the poor, Francis wanted to show others the devotion he felt towards the Infant Jesus. In the year 1223, a few weeks before Christmas, he asked a friend to make a display of the Nativity scene.

By Christmas Eve all was ready. Franciscan friars came from kilometres around to the little town of Greccio in Italy to see the first crèche. The men and women of the village lit candles and torches to

brighten the scene. The manger was made ready with straw and a life-sized wax figure of the Christ Child was placed in it. Oxen and asses were led to the spot and real people took the parts of Mary, Joseph and the shepherds. Francis stood before the crib, overcome with devotion, and a solemn Mass was sung.

The crèche and ceremony was so popular that it was not only repeated year after year, but it spread to other countries. At first only live dramas were enacted. Later miniature figures were used, generally carved from wood, but sometimes made from other materials. In France the crib scene was called a *crèche*, a name used by the English; in Italy, a *presepio*; in Spain, a *nacimiento*; and in Germany, a *Weihnachtskrippe*.

Nowadays crèches can be found at Christmas time in churches, private homes and shopping malls.

7. ADVENT

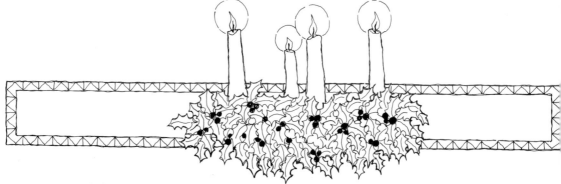

Advent, which means "coming", begins on December 1 and finishes on Christmas Day. In the Church, this is the time when people fast and pray while remembering the long journey that Joseph and Mary made to Bethlehem. In many churches, candles are lit on the four Sundays before Christmas to emphasise the advent, or coming, of the Lord.

To remind people of the Advent season, special decorations are made and hung. A German custom is the making of an Advent crown. This is a wreath of evergreens hung from the ceiling and decorated with four candles. One of these candles is lit on each of the Sundays until Christmas, so that all are alight on the fourth Sunday. The Christmas wreath hung on your front door is similar to the Advent crown.

Another decoration is the Advent calendar. The early calendars had pictures with twenty-four windows cut into them. Behind each window was a small gift or sweet. Today's Advent calendars have pictures behind the windows. The last picture is always the Nativity scene. It is opened on Christmas Day.

A similar decoration is the Advent house. It is made of cardboard. If you open a window each day of the Advent weeks, you will find a Scripture verse.

During Advent, groups of people celebrate the "coming" by carol-singing and collecting money for their church.

8. EPIPHANY

In Greek, the word epiphany means "manifestation" or "showing". The coming of the Magi to Bethlehem to worship the Christ Child is said to be one way in which Christ revealed Himself to the world as the Son of God.

Epiphany is celebrated on January 6. In the early days, in the East and in Egypt and Greece, this was the date of a pagan festival associated with rivers and water gods. Today it is a great feast day in Italy, Spain and many other countries. This is the time when children in these places are given presents in memory of the gifts brought by the Magi to baby Jesus. In Spain and France, the children go out to look for the Magi, taking gifts of hay for their camels.

In France and other countries, families used to have a Three Kings Cake with a bean hidden in it. Whoever got the slice with the bean in it was made king or queen for the day.

Another name for Epiphany is Twelfth Day. It is the last of the Twelve Days of Christmas which used to be one long holiday. It was also the last night of the Festival of Fools before the Lord of Misrule had to give up his crown and become a servant again.

Twelfth Night is the time when Christmas decorations should be taken down or they will bring bad luck. In some cities in America, the people collect all the old trees and burn them on a huge bonfire.

9. CHRISTMAS LEGENDS

Over the centuries many legends that are linked with Christmas have come into being. Here are a few of them:

Joseph and the Cherry Tree

A legend that goes back five centuries or more tells of Joseph as an old man walking with Mary in a cherry orchard. When Mary told him of the angel's visit proclaiming Christ's birth, Joseph became suspicious. He refused to pick cherries for her so she asked the branches of the tree to bend over for her. When Joseph saw this miracle, he begged her forgiveness for not believing her.

Talking Animals

Some people believe that at midnight on Christmas Eve strange things happen to animals. Cattle and horses kneel and face towards Jesus' birthplace, Bethlehem. Bees hum the Hundredth Psalm in their hives. In some European countries, animals are said to have the gift of speech. However, it is supposed to be dangerous for human beings to listen to their talk.

Legend has it that a raven was the first bird to know that Christ was born. It was flying over the Bethlehem fields when angels filled the sky. However, it was the rooster which was the first bird to tell of the event, crying "Christus natus est" (Christ is born). Since then roosters have crowed all through Christmas Eve night.

The Christmas Rose

It is said that a little shepherd girl of Bethlehem followed the shepherds who were travelling to the manger after hearing the angel's message. All the shepherds had gifts for the Christ Child, but the girl had none. This made her very sad. Suddenly, in a flash of blinding light, an angel appeared, scattering beautiful white roses in her path. The girl gathered the roses and laid them at the manger as her gift to the baby Jesus.

In medieval times the Christmas rose was considered sacred and was used to ward off the plague.

Christmas Tree Tinsel

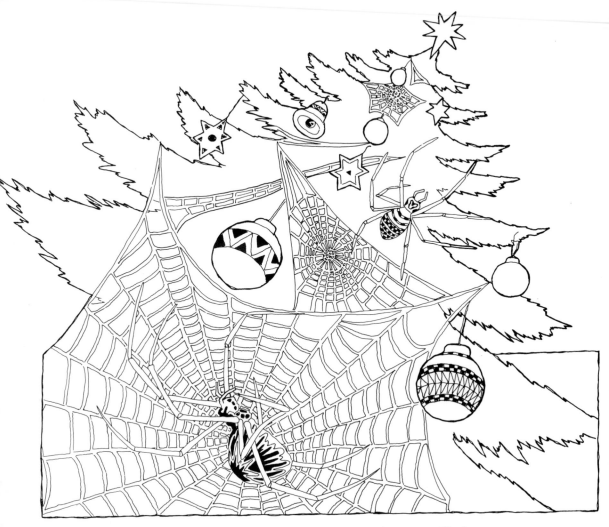

Have you ever wondered why we use tinsel to decorate Christmas trees? A legend explains it this way: many years ago a good woman with a large family of children decorated her tree one Christmas Eve. During the night, spiders crawled from branch to branch of the tree, spinning their webs. To reward the mother for her kindness, the Christ Child blessed the tree and all the spider webs were turned into shining silver.

10. A NATIVITY PLAY

The First Christmas

Dianne Bates

Characters:
Joseph
Mary
King Herod
Roman officer
Page
Courtiers
Three Wise Man (Magi)
Five Shepherds
Villagers
Choir of angels

Note: If possible, all action should take place in front of the curtain until the final scene.

Enter the choir to the music of "Mary's Boy Child". A soloist sings this song with the choir humming in the background.

Scene: *Nazareth, at the home of Joseph and Mary. Mary is seated. Enter Joseph.*

Joseph: Mary, it seems we must go to the city of David, the place of my ancestor, for so has Augustus Caesar decreed it. There is to be an enrolment and all must go.

Mary: My good husband, it is as though the prophet Micah and the angel Gabriel's forecasts are to come true. Our son is to be born in Bethlehem – future ruler of Israel as Micah foretold ...

Joseph: ... and Son of God, the Saviour of all people ...

Mary: ... and King forever and ever, as the angel Gabriel proclaimed. How blessed we are, Joseph.

Joseph: The journey is only four days hence, but it will be hard on you, my dear wife, with our child to be born so soon.

Mary: I shall ride upon the donkey. It will be no burden. Come, we must waste no more time.

Exit. Choir sings "Hark! The Herald Angels Sing".

Scene: *King Herod's court. Drum roll. Herod enters, followed by a Roman officer. He sits upon his throne.*

Officer: There are three Magi in the outer court, awaiting your pleasure, Herod. They say they have been led to Jerusalem by a star from the East, a star that tells of the birth of the King of the Jews.
Herod: I am the only king! There is no other king but me.
Officer: Indeed you are King of Judea. But always, like me, you are servant of our master, Augustus Caesar.

Enter courtiers, bowing to Herod. Then enter a page, followed by the Magi.

Page: Sire, I present the three Magi from the East.
1st Wise Man: Greetings, Herod, King of Judea, from us all.
Herod: Yes, yes ... I hear you are here in search of another king, King of the Jews.
2nd Wise Man: This is true, oh mighty Herod. For we have seen his star in the East and have come to worship him.
3rd Wise Man: As the prophets foretold, the king we seek is to be found in your land.

Herod: I am the only king in Judea!

1st Wise Man: Is not Augustus Caesar of Rome, king of this land? His soldiers are everywhere within this palace.

Officer: Augustus, Emperor of Rome, master of the world, is King Herod's master and protector.

Herod: But I am king in this country. Who are you to come to my court and dispute this?

1st Wise Man: We are Magi from the East. Wise men, people call us.

2nd Wise Man: We study the stars, and they have shown us that the King of Kings is born in this land. He shall have far greater power than ever shall have Augustus Caesar.

Officer: This shall never be! No one has more power than the Emperor of all the world. Beware of how you speak in the presence of a Roman officer!

3rd Wise Man: We speak only the truth as we know it.

Herod: You talk not like wise men, but like fools! But then, I challenge you ... go, follow this star further. See if you can find this mighty king.

1st Wise Man: Herod is gracious.

2nd Wise Man: We thank you, sire.

Herod: But listen on. If you should find him, return to me. If this King of Kings does exist – and I think you wrong – but if he does, then I wish to know where to find him.

Officer: You heard Herod. You are to return with the news. Augustus Caesar will need to know if there be any other kings in this part of the world.

3rd Wise Man: We shall do as you ask, Herod.

1st Wise Man: Fare thee well, sire. We shall return.

Exit, followed by page and courtiers.

Herod: Have your men follow them, captain. Find this king of whom they speak.

Officer: They are, as you said, only fools. Fools from the East. What would they know?

Herod: Do as I command! For many years the prophets have told of the King of the Jews. They may be right. And if they are, I shall find this king and murder him. Just as surely as I murdered members of my own family when they crossed me.

Officer: I shall send my men straight away. (*Exit.*)

Choir sings first verse and chorus of "We Three Kings". Enter the three kings from one side of the stage, and the shepherds from the other.

1st Wise Man: Greetings, men of Bethlehem!

1st Shepherd: Greetings, strangers.

2nd Wise Man: Who might you be?

2nd Shepherd: We are but humble shepherds, sir.

3rd Shepherd: But we have been visited by an angel as we watched our sheep on the hills of Bethlehem . . .

4th Shepherd: . . . and taken to the Saviour, who is Christ the Lord.

3rd Wise Man: But *we* are in search of this Lord.

2nd Wise Man: We have brought him gifts – gold, frankincense and myrrh.

1st Wise Man: We have seen his birth written in the heavens.

2nd Wise Man: Look, the star has stopped!

3rd Wise Man: Our long journey has come to an end.

5th Shepherd: The star stops above the stable wherein is the Christ Child.

1st Wise Man: The king born in a stable?

1st Shepherd: And a manger for his bed, sir.

2nd Wise Man: We can delay no longer. Will you lead the way, brother?

2nd Shepherd: The great rich man called me "brother"!

2nd Wise Man: Tonight we are all brothers as we meet with Christ the Saviour.

3rd Wise Man: Let us all go in and see this Saviour.

Curtains open to reveal the Nativity scene. Mary is seated near the manger with Jesus in her arms. Joseph stands beside her. Villagers stand around them both. The kings move forward to present their gifts while the shepherds look on. Choir sings "Away in a Manger". During this, the Officer enters, stands and watches.

Officer: It *is* true. As the prophets told, a king born in Bethlehem, and the wise men offer him gifts.

1st Shepherd (to Officer): We shepherds heard the angels speaking the words of the prophets. We did as they told and came here with haste to find Mary and Joseph, and the babe lying in the manger.

1st Wise Man: Now we must return to Herod and tell him of the new king.

Officer: No, you must not!

1st Wise Man: But why must we not?

Officer: Herod has sworn to murder the child.

2nd Wise Man: I dreamed only last night of Herod slaying many children.

Officer: You must take heed of your dream. Go home another way. Do not delay, for he will surely send others after you.

3rd Wise Man: But you are one of Herod's men. How do we know you speak the truth?

Officer: As I stood here, watching the babe, a great spirit entered me. And now, with all my heart and soul, I wish to serve this new Lord and King.

1st Wise Man: There is no doubt – he speaks with sincerity. Let us all praise the new Lord!

Chorus: Praise the Lord!

All step back so the Nativity scene is in full view. Some bow, others kneel in homage. The choir hums the first verse of "O Come, All Ye Faithful", then all join in the chorus and the remaining verses. The curtains close when the song finishes.

END

INDEX